THE LESSER OF TWO EVILS

You've pondered *If....* You've found all the answers to *The Book of Questions*. You've mastered *Six Degrees of Kevin Bacon*. Now it's time to really search your mind . . .

Would you rather . . .

be able to give change for a dollar by putting it in your mouth
or
be capable of shifting the part in your hair by instructing it vocally?

Would you rather . . .

watch a porno movie with your parents
or
watch a porno movie starring your parents?

Would you rather . . .

have a city named after you
or
have a professional wrestler base his gimmick on impersonating you?

Over 200
Absolutely
Absurd
Dilemmas
to Ponder

WOULD YOU RATHER . . . ?

Justin Heimberg & David Gomberg

 A PLUME BOOK

PLUME
Published by the Penguin Group
Penguin Putnam Inc., 375 Hudson Street, New York, New York 10014, U.S.A.
Penguin Books Ltd, 27 Wrights Lane, London W8 5TZ, England
Penguin Books Australia Ltd, Ringwood, Victoria, Australia
Penguin Books Canada Ltd, 10 Alcorn Avenue, Toronto, Ontario, Canada M4V 3B2
Penguin Books (N.Z.) Ltd, 182–190 Wairau Road, Auckland 10, New Zealand

Penguin Books Ltd, Registered Offices:
Harmondsworth, Middlesex, England

First published by Plume, an imprint of Dutton Signet,
a member of Penguin Putnam Inc.

First Printing, September, 1997

19 20

 REGISTERED TRADEMARK—MARCA REGISTRADA

CIP data is available.

ISBN 0-452-27851-1

Printed in the United States of America
Set in Serifa Roman
Designed by Jesse Cohen

BOOKS ARE AVAILABLE AT QUANTITY DISCOUNTS WHEN USED TO PROMOTE PRODUCTS OR SERVICES. FOR INFORMATION PLEASE WRITE TO PREMIUM MARKETING DIVISION, PENGUIN PUTNAM INC., 375 HUDSON STREET, NEW YORK, NEW YORK 10014.

To 82 Ulster

ACKNOWLEDGMENTS

Thanks first to our families for all of their encouragement and support throughout our lives. Thanks to Jay Mandel for his sage advice, sense of humor, and incredibly strange handwriting. And thanks of course to Danielle Perez and Eben Weiss for all of their help, and for tolerating our unhealthy obsession with former NBA seven footers.

We would also like to recognize the contributions of Jason Heimberg, Matt Scharf, Paul Katz, Eric Grunspan, Dave Miller, Todd DeHart, Grimaldi, Kurt Mease, Eric Gomberg (who knew how to spell "Lipps, Inc."), Jon Grunspan, Eric Sarin, Jon Tabor, Jen Thompson, and Sank. Lastly, we would like to acknowledge the existence of Eric David Kesselman.

ABOUT THE AUTHORS

PHOTOS: SUSANNAH MEADOWS

JUSTIN HEIMBERG

DAVID GOMBERG

Would you rather be . . .

Justin Heimberg, a 5'8"–5'9" half-Jewish guy with the spark-plug physique, who poses for photographs with an artificially forlorn look in his eyes

or

David Gomberg, a 6'2" lanky guy with bad knees whose gleaming smile belies severe existential angst and inner turmoil?

Things to consider: Justin Heimberg and David Gomberg both graduated from Duke University in 1995; Gomberg with a degree in philosophy and Heimberg with a B.A. Baracus in English. Gomberg currently works for NEXTOY, a toy development company, while Heimberg is considering a career in what he calls "functional performance art," where he performs mundane chores while rendering his unique style of spoken word.

Check out our website at www.wouldyourather.com

DISACKNOWLEDGMENTS

e would like to disacknowledge that lady in the bookstore who always told us "This isn't a library," that guy who wouldn't give us a falafel parmigiana for absolutely no reason, and Jeff Leavitt.

CONTENTS

A NOTE FROM THE AUTHORS

Two years ago, we were struck with a vision. The vision: to develop the perfect socially interactive book, a book that would bring people together, ignite the imagination, and induce furious fits of laughter. So we set off to work, and after countless late nights of strain and struggle, we completed our final draft. It consisted of forty blank pages and a bottle of gin. Unfortunately, we couldn't find a publisher, and we were forced to move on to other projects. Our next two books, *120 Things You Can Do with a Salmon* and *Scott Baio and the Western World*, while embraced in certain academic circles, failed to excite the public's attention. But we refused to be discouraged, and after consulting more than five hundred Ph.D.'s, various heads of state, and a number of prominent religious leaders, we created *Would You Rather . . . ?*

This is not a book about values. Don't get us wrong. We have nothing against values. Some of our best friends have values. But this is not a book about them. Indeed, *Would You Rather . . . ?* is not particularly taxing on the conscience, but rather simply seeks to entertain with over two hundred "of the most difficult choices you'll never have to make." Often, the dilemmas place you between the rockiest of rocks and the hardest of hard places; always, the alternatives are hilariously absurd. To use this book, simply read a question aloud to a group of friends and thoroughly debate the alternatives until each of you arrives at a decision. Bear in mind: You must choose! That's the whole point of this thing. Once everyone has chosen, move on and tackle the next question. If you have no friends, it's okay because the book is funny enough to be read alone.

On occasion we've provided a few things to consider when deliberating a question. But don't feel restricted to discussing the questions solely in terms of what we have provided, as half the fun lies in imagining the many ways your life will be affected after making your choice. We promise you that the other pages in the book will have significantly fewer words on them, so turn the page, read on, and embarrass yourself by laughing aloud in a public place.

CHAPTER 1

You've Been Cursed!

These are the circumstances. A powerful deity descends from on high and informs you that, for reasons beyond your understanding, you must live out the remainder of your life plagued with a terrible curse—a bizarre behavioral disorder, an outrageous physical deformity, an irksome inconvenience, etc. The deity is not without compassion, however. He allows you to choose between two possible fates.

Would you rather . . .
have living eyebrows that crawl about your face
or
leave a trail of paprika wherever you go?

Would you rather . . .

appear as Yasir Arafat in the mirror

or

have a bizarre neurological condition where anytime you enter a room, Darth Vader's theme sounds?

Things to consider: shaving, dating, public rest rooms

Would you rather . . .

briefly turn into Dom DeLuise every forty-five minutes

or

have skin fifteen times bigger than it needs to be?

Things to consider: the repercussions on your wardrobe, playing sports, sex life

Would you rather . . .
have your eyes and nipples switch places

or

your nose and perineum? (Look it up.)

Would you rather . . .

never have had your umbilical cord disconnected from your mother

or

have had it disconnected but reconnected to Soupy Sales? Things to consider: pick-up basketball games, married life, is Soupy still alive?

Would you rather . . .

have a sinus infection where anytime you sneeze while in the presence of others, they change sex

or

have the inability to distinguish between babies and English muffins?

Things to consider: grocery shopping, buttering, watching a football game during allergy season

Would you rather . . .

have a digitally blurred face like criminals on TV

or

have your range of bodily movement reduced to that of a G.I. Joe action figure?

Things to consider: brushing your teeth, cocktail parties

Would you rather . . .

have to shower and bathe daily with a hippopotamus (the hippopotamus is not dangerous)

or

have to live with former NBA great Ralph Sampson? (Sampson is not dangerous.)

Would you rather . . .
urinate through your nose

or

smell things with your genitalia?

Would you rather . . .

collect lint at ten thousand times your natural rate?

or

have everything you do in life relayed out loud by Marv Albert?

Things to consider: taking a shower, sexual advances, the average American accrues one quarter pound of lint a day

Would you rather . . .

have to sleep each night between a mattress and a box spring

or

be allowed to listen to only one musical piece the rest of your life—"Funkytown" by Lipps, Inc.

Things to consider: your wedding day, your wedding night

Would you rather . . .

have an invariable tendency to introduce yourself and others in the voice and style of a professional wrestling announcer (e.g., "From parts unknown, at 155 pounds . . .")

or

have your legal name changed to Pumpy?

Things to consider: job applications, job interviews

Would you rather . . .

emit the smell of sulfur every time you smile

or

cry glue?

Would you rather . . .

have the head of Herve Villeches (*Fantasy Island*'s Tattoo) in place of your left hand, and the head of Ricardo Montalban (*Fantasy Island*'s Mr. Rourke) in place of your right hand

or

be unable to go places without an entourage of bickering Vietnamese politicians?

Things to consider: taking the subway, boxing, airports

Would you rather have . . .

bendy straws for hair or newspaper for skin?

pork chops for earlobes or magic eight balls for elbows?

Crayolas for teeth or shrimp for nipples?

Would you rather . . .
be restricted in writing utensils to lip balm

or

be plagued with the inescapable and involuntary tendency to insert the word "bucket" as every other word you say? Example: "Hey bucket, Seth. Bucket, how've bucket you bucket been?"

Would you rather . . .
belch the sound of a gong
or
sneeze the sound of a bowling strike?

Would you rather . . .
vomit marbles
or
sweat cheese?
Things to consider: projectile vomiting, jogging, the flu

Would you rather . . .

have skin that doesn't tan upon direct contact with sunlight, but rather plaids

or

have a vocal cord deformity whereupon attempting to utter any type of greeting, the *Happy Days* theme blasts from your mouth?

Would you rather . . .
eat by putting food down your pants

or

not?

Workin' for the Man

The deity has decided it's time for a career change. Permanent and full-time.

Would you rather be . . .
a toll booth operator

or

the guy who mops up at X-rated movie houses?

Would you rather be . . .
the guy on an assembly line who stamps the price tag on a bag of pretzels, fourteen hours a day

or

Richard Simmons' personal assistant?

Would you rather be . . .

a member of an Amish collective farm

or

a professional wrestler called "The Tailor" whose gimmick is to alter wrestlers' trunks after pin-fall?

Would you rather be . . .

a super-villain called "The Pharmacist"

or

the god of upholstery?

Would you rather be . . .

a marine with scant bladder control

or

a chess grandmaster with Tourette's syndrome?

CHAPTER

Sex

Content with your sex life? Well, the deity isn't, and for reasons beyond your understanding, it's imperative that he spices it up. But how? A hang-up? A fetish? A mandatory feat of perverted passion? There are so many ways for a nearly omnipotent deity to meddle with your love life, and there's nothing you can do about it. You need not feel entirely powerless, of course. Once again you may (and must) choose between two possible fates.

Would you rather . . .

be unable to perform sexually unless witnessed by a major league baseball umpire

or

have daily phone sex with Henry Kissinger?

Would you rather . . .

watch a porno movie with your parents

or

watch a porno movie starring your parents?

Would you rather . . .

have sex with a four foot tall woman or a seven foot tall woman? 3'2" or 8'1"? 1'3" or 10'6"?

or

have sex with a four foot tall man or an eight foot tall man? 3'4" or 8'9"? 2'3" or 9'10"?

Would you rather . . .

have sexual organs that glow red like ET's heart when you're attracted to someone

or

have the faint sound of playground chatter perpetually emanating from your crotch?

Things to consider: funerals, wearing white pants, oral sex

Would you rather have sex with . . .

John Sununu or Mr. T.?

Don King or Gerald Ford?

Bill Gates or Sinbad?

Boris Yeltsin or the guy who played Horshack on *Welcome Back, Kotter*?

Siskel or Ebert?

Ernie or Bert?

Would you rather have sex with ...
Martina Navratilova or Barbara Walters?

Ginger or Mary-Anne?

Nancy Reagan or Cindy Crawford if she was missing an arm? Both arms? And a leg? Just a torso and a head?

Bea Arthur or Aunt Jemima?

Tammy-Fae Baker or a mahogany coat rack?

Would you rather . . .

have sultry porno movie music sound out whenever you make a romantic advance

or

lose all sexual inhibition in the presence of cantaloupe?

Things to consider: possible X-rated film career, fruit salad at Grandma's

Would you . . .
have sex with Jesse Helms to have sex with Brad Pitt?

Would you . . .
have sex with Jesse Helms to have sex with Pamela Anderson?

Would you . . .
have sex with all of the Supreme Court justices in order to earn the official title of "Cap'n"?

Would you rather . . .

have an incredibly adhesive face

or

have a mildly magnetic scrotum (men); magnetic breasts (women)?

Things to consider: kissing, metal benches, zippers

Sex

Would you rather . . .

never have sex again

or

have sex once with a walrus?

Things to consider: ever increasing irritability, tusks

Would you rather . . .
never have sex again
or
have sex once with *the* Walrus?

Would you rather . . .

require instructional flow charts to successfully partake in foreplay

or

be plagued with impure thoughts about Gene Shalit?

Things to consider: ruining the mood, Gene Shalit!

Would you rather . . .

experience orgasm upon hearing the word "pancake"

or

reflexively belt out the chorus of "Come on, Eileen" upon reaching climax?

Things to consider: family brunches, breakfast at IHOP

Would you rather . . .

be unable to undress yourself without the aid of former Milwaukee Buck Paul Mokeski

or

have optic nerve damage which causes your partner to appear as Mao Tse Tung during sex?

Would you rather . . .

administer a "BJ" to every member of the Oakridge Boys

or

be double-teamed by Grimace and Mayor McCheese?

Things to consider: the Oakridge Boys' enchanting harmonies, special sauce, Grimace's tremendous staying power

Would you rather . . .

have sex in front of your parents

or

have sex in front of twenty thousand-plus screaming professional wrestling fans?

Things to consider: the shame you'll feel if the fans chant, "Bor-ing. Bor-ing." The shame you'll feel if your parents chant, "Bor-ing. Bor-ing."

Would you rather . . .

have your partner's sexual appetite vary directly with the Miami Dolphins' road record

or

be found sexually attractive only by meteorologists?
Things to consider: the aging Dan Marino, the irrepressible Al Roker

Would you rather . . .

have sex with Mel Gibson and get mono

or

have sex with Pat Sajak and get a really cool pair of overalls that you really wanted?

Would you rather . . .

have your romantic moments scored by an Air Supply soundtrack

or

make the sounds of a pinball machine during intercourse?

Would you rather . . .

have sex with Tom Bosley and receive 15,000 dollars' worth of non-redeemable arcade tokens

or

have sex with Tom Cruise and get a venereal disease called "Pubic Elves" where little men infest your crotch area, leaving nothing but a sparkling green rash?

Sex

Would you rather . . .

have seventeen testicles

or

just one testicle the size of a coconut?

Would you rather . . .

be able to give other people orgasms simply by clapping your hands

or

regularly attend orgies with the Superfriends?

Things to consider: Wondertwin powers, Batman's utility belt, Aquaman's flounder fetish (AFF)

Crampin' Your Style!

The deity, being the fashion-conscious super-being he is, isn't happy with your style. Those Jams and that Spuds Mackenzie cap just aren't cutting it anymore. Let's get with the times.

Would you rather . . .
have no hair on your face and head where you are supposed to have hair, and hair on your face where you are not supposed to have hair

or

be allowed to wear only one outfit, a suit with the faces of all the vice-presidents on it?

Would you rather . . .
have a receding hair line

or

a **PRO**ceding hair line?

Would you rather . . .

have to sport a key-chain nipple ring

or

have a wardrobe that consists entirely of outfits worn by the Scooby Doo characters?

Things to consider: Fred's neckerchief, unlocking your car door

Would you rather . . .

have a life-size tattoo of Andy Griffith on your back

or

be permitted to use only one deodorant scent: sour cream and chives?

Would you rather have to always wear . . .
moon boots or a sombrero?

Ferrari glasses or knee-high tube socks?

orthodontic head gear or two left shoes?

vestigial wings or Fudgeboots®?

3

Not-Quite-Super Powers

You've caught the deity in a good mood. He decides that you deserve a break and offers you the chance to live the rest of your life blessed with a special ability—a power, a gift of sorts. He even gives you a say in the matter, allowing you to choose between two possible fortunate fates.

Would you rather . . .
be able to give change for a dollar by putting it in your mouth

or

be capable of shifting the part in your hair by instructing it vocally?

Would you rather . . .
have skin that tans upon hearing the voice of Al Gore

or

be able to make Amish people break-dance?

Would you rather . . .
have the power to shave just by thinking really hard
or
have an unexplainable gift, whereupon flushing the toilet,
everybody in the building renounces their religion?
Things to consider: impressing dates, bar mitzvahs

Would you rather . . .

have increased charm when on the Tundra

or

have unquestionable priority when it comes to using mutual armrests in public theaters?

Would you rather . . .

be able to expedite the arrival of an elevator by pressing the
button multiple times

or

have the ability to sound incredibly natural and sincere on
an answering machine?

Would you rather . . .
have retractable claws
or
prehensile dreadlocks?

Would you rather . . .

be impervious to the red-eye phenomenon in photographs

or

have expert precision when straw-puncturing Capri Sun pouches?

Would you rather . . .

be able to teleport one inch forward

or

have an echo that is in the voice of Edward G. Robinson?

Would you rather . . .
be able to walk on pudding

or

be able to project holograms of Mexican super-group Menudo?

Things to consider: street performing, convincing primitive cultures you're a god

Would you rather . . .
have a ketchup-dispensing navel

or

a pencil-sharpening nostril?

Would you rather . . .
be able to communicate with the dead, but have to converse solely in jive

or

have a "save game" function for your life?

Would you rather . . .
be able to turn water into Colt .45
or
be able to summon the Baldwin brothers?

Would you rather . . .
have superior diplomatic skills when negotiating lunch-food trades
or
know how to say "Where's the beef?" in over three hundred languages?

Would you rather . . .

have glow-in-the-dark body hair

or

be immune to the lethal combination of Pop Rocks and Coke?

Things to consider: completely gratuitous reference to "Pop Rocks and Coke" myth

Would you rather . . .

be able to do a perfect impression of Cab Calloway

or

be irresistible to people with the surname "Fishbein"?

Things to consider: (a) When's the last time you saw an attractive Fishbein? (b) Teri Hatcher's real name is Teri Fishbein (so they say). And (c) If you can do a perfect impression of Cab Calloway, you're probably going to be irresistible to Fishbeins anyway.

Would you rather . . .

be able to successfully avoid doing chores and facing minor relationship problems by hiding under some coats for a little while

or

be able to bake chicken pot pie in your pants?

Gifts Aplenty!

The deity is feeling charitable. He has a few old deity things in his old deity garage that he needs to get rid of, and guess what? You're the lucky beneficiary!

Would you rather have . . .

a voodoo doll of Saddam Hussein

or

an inflatable doll of Rerun from *What's Happening!!*?
Things to consider: effects on Middle East peace process, fun in the pool

Would you rather have . . .

Cindy Crawford as your personal sex slave

or

an unlimited supply of fudge?

Things to consider: likely possibility of seducing Cindy with all that fudge

Would you rather have . . .

a wallet of infinite talc

or

a regenerative meat loaf?

Would you rather receive . . .
a little bald sidekick to slap around
or
backstage passes to the Nelson concert?

Would you rather receive . . .
a goose that lays golden eggs
or
an elk that craps beat-up Buicks?

4

Deaths, Tortures, and Other Generally Unpleasant Stuff

Unfortunately, we all must die and, in many of the following cases, suffer a horrible death of incredibly unnatural causes. Why? Reasons beyond your understanding. Of course, not all of the following choices concern death. Sometimes it is a painful torture you must suffer or a repulsive and dangerous act that you must commit. ☺

Would you rather . . .
swallow a dozen thumbtacks

or

cut off your lower lip with a rusty pair of scissors?

Would you rather . . .
consume fifteen pounds of raw bacon

or

bathe twice in a tub of bile?

Would you rather . . .
be hole-punched to death

or

be eaten alive by the cast of *Diff'rent Strokes*?
Things to consider: the delightful Gary Coleman, puncture wounds

Would you rather . . .

have your left eyeball pierced with a pin

or

have your right Achilles' tendon snipped with gardening clippers?

Would you rather . . .

be stoned to death by pickles

or

be submerged in mayonnaise until you suffocate?

Would you rather . . .

have your face Krazy-glued to the underside of a Concorde

or

be trampled to death by the New Jersey Nets?

Would you rather . . . (Amish only)

get your hand caught in the butter churner

or

be forced to use ornamental buttons and zippers?

Would you rather be stuck in an elevator with . . .
sweaty sumo wrestlers or talkative accountants?

untalented impressionists or super-pretentious milkmen?

jolly contortionists or giddy rabbis?

apathetic ringmasters or sarcastic postal workers?

After you die, would you rather . . .
be buried in your high school gymnasium

or

be cremated and have your ashes sprinkled over Ted Koppel?

After you die, would you rather . . .
be preserved in ice and displayed in the House of Chinese Gourmet in Rockville, Maryland

or

have your body donated to a couple of kids in the neighborhood who think they can do "some really cool stuff"?

Would you rather . . .
be bludgeoned to death with a slab of beef
or
be trapped in a submarine until it slowly filled up with water? Vinegar? Elvis impersonators?

Would you rather . . .
have your head implode
or
have your head explode?

Would you rather . . .

notice live maggots in your Milky Way after you've eaten two big bites

or

find a few pubic hairs at the bottom of your Caesar salad?

Would you rather . . . (Orthodox Jews only)

find out you've just eaten pork

or

find out your yarmulke was used for a washcloth?

Would you rather . . .

be tenderized to death with a small wooden mallet

or

consume Kleenex until you die?

Would you rather . . .

eat a live gerbil

or

remove your own appendix with nothing but a shoe horn and a rusty old menorah?

Would you rather . . .

break a light bulb in your mouth

or

be slashed with a thousand paper cuts and then dipped into a giant bowl of rubbing alcohol?

Would you rather . . .
be able to use only one piece of tissue/napkin your whole life
or
imbibe all liquids through a fallopian tube?

Would you rather . . .
give an enema to an elephant
or
give an enema to Nipsey Russel?

Would you rather watch . . .
a man get hit by a speeding truck

or

your parents having sex?

Would you rather watch . . .
a man get hit by a speeding truck

or

your parents having a three-way with former NBA great Ralph Sampson?

Would you rather . . .
remove a thirty-foot tapeworm from a rhinoceros

or

be ejaculated on by Snuffalupagus?

Would you rather . . .
read *Hamlet*

or

give blood?

Gut-wrenchers

This time the deity is just getting off on a power trip. He wants to see you squirm and blush in utter humiliation. And thus he offers you these excruciatingly embarrassing scenarios.

Would you rather . . .
take all your showers naked in a storefront window for a month

or

masturbate in front of your fourth-grade teacher?

Would you rather . . .

gyrate spastically in front of your best friend's parents for a full two minutes

or

wear an obscenely revealing thong bathing suit to the beach?

Would you rather . . .

have your most revealing love letters published in *People*

or

have your honeymoon night broadcast on closed-circuit TV?

Would you rather . . .

have terrible gas on a first date

or

be playing kickball at a new school, and not know the lingo, and so when they ask you how you want your pitch, you mutter in a shaking, trembling voice, "Soft and nutty," and you should have said, "Slow and smooth," and so they laugh at you and the girls hate you and Ricky Ordonez beats the crap out of you?

Would you rather . . .

have just given the greatest speech of your life only to realize that your zipper was down the whole time

or

just confessed your love for someone over the phone only to find out that on the other line wasn't your beloved but rather former NBA great Ralph Sampson?

CHAPTER 5

Would You Rather Live in a World Where . . .

We all want to change the world, but alas, we seldom can. There is, however, a certain deity that you may have heard of with that kind of power. And this particular deity, on this particular day, is indeed going to change the world, for better or for worse. And for reasons that perhaps only Sinbad can understand, you have the final say!

Would you rather live in a world ...

where the handshake was replaced by the act of grabbing another's genitals, giggling, and bouncing up and down

or

where all international disputes were settled by means of break-dancing contests?

Would you rather live in a world . . .

where massive Afros were mandatory for members of Congress

or

where it was legal, in fact encouraged, to crucify mimes?

Would you rather live in a world . . .

where Underoos were standard business attire

or

where rabbi and professional bowler was one job?

Would you rather live in a world . . .

where the dominant milieu for social interaction was not the bar scene, but rather intense games of dodge ball

or

where humans sniffed each other like dogs?

Would you rather live in . . .
the Star Trek universe
or
the world of Dr. Seuss?

Would you rather live in . . .
a Salvador Dali landscape
or
Tolkien's Middle Earth?

Would you rather live in . . .
biblical Palestine
or
the world of Atari's Berserk?
Things to consider: Is there really a difference?

Would you rather live in a world . . .
where it snowed ground beef

or

where everybody looked like Phil Bautista?
Things to consider: clean-up, sledding, wanted posters

Would you rather live in a world . . .
where everybody's speech was badly dubbed over like in a Chinese kung-fu movie

or

where golfer Craig Stadler was hailed as our overlord?

Would you rather live in a world . . .

where at the end of a rainbow there really was a pot of gold

or

where at the end of a rainbow there were five hundred cases of Pabst Blue Ribbon?

Would you rather live in a world . . .

where there was no such thing as war, but also no such thing as pork

or

where there was no such thing as crime, but also no such thing as the A-Team?

Would you rather live in a world . . .

where all dirty words and vulgar expressions were censored with silly bleeps, buzzes, and cuckoos

or

where professional wrestling was rightfully considered the apex of human thought and accomplishment?

Would you rather live in a world (nerds only) . . .

where computer gaming was a lucrative and respected sport

or

where it was legally enforced to have Dungeons and Dragons statistics on your driver's license?

Would you rather live in a world . . .
where people's heights fluctuated significantly from day to day

or

where their ages did?

Would you rather live in a country . . .
where the national currency was the Nilla Wafer

or

where the national anthem was Quiet Riot's "Cum on Feel the Noize"?

Things to consider: ATMs, Olympics

Go to Hell!

You have been sent directly to Hell. Do not pass go. Do not collect $200.

Would you rather be sentenced to . . .
a gridlocked traffic jam with literally no end

or

an eternal bar-mitzvah party where a painfully bad band sings "Celebration" and "Shout" over and over?

Would you rather be sentenced to . . .
a permanent ice cream headache

or

a never-ending lecture entitled "Fabio: Cross-cultural Perspectives"?

Would you rather be sentenced to . . .

eternal Stairmaster

or

perpetual diarrhea?

Things to consider: Which do you think is the better band name?

CHAPTER 6
Mixed Blessings

You must have caught the oh-so-moody deity in mid-mood swing. For the deity, in all his benevolence, feels that along with a horrible curse, you deserve a wonderful blessing. Of course, this makes choosing that much more difficult.

Would you rather . . .

be able to draw like Picasso but smell intensely of raspberry

or

be able to compose like Mozart but have to always wear those really dark, tight designer jeans from the seventies?

Would you rather . . .

have a fifty-inch vertical leap but swell up around the neck and face when storms are brewing

or

have baby-soft skin but have to carry a picture of Leonard Nimoy in your wallet?

Would you rather . . .

have the wit of Rosie O'Donnell and the voice of Rosie Perez

or

the hair of Tom Snyder and the voice of Tom Carvel?

Would you rather . . .

have perfectly developed trapezius muscles but shaky moral grounding

or

be able to generate complex shadow puppets but comprehend absolutely nothing said to you between the hours of three and four p.m.?

Would you rather . . .

have the voice of Barry White but have the face of Barry Goldwater

or

have the body of Bob Packwood but the face of Ms. Pac-Man?

Would you rather ...
be good with computers but have an incredibly moist left foot

or

be regarded as the greatest diorama maker of all time but have a friendly midget permanently strapped to you, papoose style?

Would you rather . . .

have a moderate stutter but unlimited credit at Foot Locker

or

have a good short-term memory but always tack on a real
sarcastic "Einstein" at the end of any compliment?

Would you rather . . .

have a flair for interior design but wobble ceaselessly in the presence of small children

or

be able to type eighty words a minute but moan like Chewbacca when you defecate?

Things to consider: public rest rooms, domestic life

Would you rather . . .

become increasingly intelligent with the consumption of alcohol, but also become increasingly convinced you are Gloria Estefan

or

have a firm grasp of Roman numerals but look exactly like Weird Al Yankovic?

Things to consider: nightclubs, karaoke, yellow knee pads

Would you rather . . .

have a firm grasp of fly fishing but always mispronounce the word *nuclear*

or

be fluent in Japanese but explode on July 17, 2032?

Would you rather . . .

have the body of a ninety-year old and the mind of a thirty-year old

or

the mind of a ninety-year old and the body of the fat guy from *Head of the Class*?

Would you rather . . .

be lactose intolerant but be proficient as a human beat box

or

have to wear a retainer but know exactly when to hold them, exactly when to fold them, and precisely the moments where you should simply walk away?

Would You Rather ... for Beginners

Would you rather ...
have terrible burn scars
or

a cute button nose?

Would you rather ...
be in perfect physical shape
or

be fat and bald, with a dumpy spark-plug physique?

Would you rather ...
coast through life, catching all the breaks
or

suffer miserably, and die dejected and brokenhearted?

CHAPTER 7
Wishful Thinking

It's your lucky day. The deity has decided to help make one of your wildest fantasies come true. . . . Well, maybe not your wildest.

Would you rather . . .
punch Mussolini
or
tickle Rip Taylor?

Would you rather . . .

have a pile-on with the cast of *Golden Girls*

or

play a game of racquetball with Harriet Tubman?
Things to consider: Tubman's overhead smash

Would you rather . . .

never have a bad hair day

or

be allowed one do-over when you screw up while trying to pick up men/women?

Would you rather . . .

be able to clearly elucidate the differences between Doric, Ionic, and Corinthian columns

or

have all people who do that rounded up and destroyed?

Would you rather . . .

go fishing with Uncle Ben

or

lambada with Uncle Jesse?

Would you rather . . .
have a city named after you

or

a professional wrestler base his gimmick on impersonating you?

Would you rather . . .
split a bottle of whiskey with Jimmy Carter

or

be related to Charo?

Would you rather . . .
have your face on the ten-dollar bill
or
Jimmy Walker's face?

Would you rather have complete control over . . .

every headline of the *New York Times*

or

who mates with whom?

Would you rather have complete control over . . .

who gets elected to all offices

or

who wins all sporting championships?

Things to consider: President Goldthwait, Senator Boesch, Deputy Mirsky

Would you rather have complete control over . . .
who gets to go to Heaven and Hell
or
who gets to star in movies?

Would you rather . . .
win the Nobel prize for physics
or
be the World Wrestling Federation heavyweight champion?

Would you rather . . .
have toast with Napoleon
or
hold hands with Trent Tucker?

Would you rather spend a day with . . .
Shakespeare or Benny Hill?

Van Gogh or Elvis?

Jesus or Tom Kite?

Would you rather . . .
be double-jointed
or
have near invincibility at Connect Four?

Would you rather . . .

install the Clapper at the next State of the Union address

or

slip LSD into Judge Wapner's drink shortly before he hears a case?

Would you rather hear . . .
Ray Charles sing in Yiddish

or

Jessie Jackson read aloud from *Penthouse Forum*?

Would you rather . . .
be able to comprehend the most complicated theories of modern physics

or

be the best country-line dancer in the world?

Would you rather . . .
play a game of basketball with Michael Jordan

or

meet the man who engineered Carvel ice cream cakes Cookie-Puss and Fudgie the Whale?

Would You Rather . . . ʃ that Didn't Make It into the Book

Throughout the creative process we—or the deity, we should say—came up with many ideas that were too insipid, too infantile, or too tasteless to make it into the book. Here are a few examples.

Would you rather . . .
be 6'2" 200 lbs.
or
6'3" 203 lbs.?

Would you rather . . .
go to the store
or
borrow the milk?

Would you rather . . .
find a Weeble in your bowel movement
or
vice-versa?

Would you rather . . .
be unaffected by the Higgs Field—a theoretical superforce
that permeates the universe, endowing matters with mass
or
fart confetti?

CHAPTER 8
The Deity's Greatest Hits

The deity has been sniffing glue, and in his Elmer's-induced stupor he sets himself on the randomest of random play. You have no idea what kind of quandary you're about to face.

Would you rather . . .

have a variety of dyslexia where anything you try to read becomes a page from *Yes, I Can*, the story of Sammy Davis, Jr.

or

have a bizarre sleep disorder where you always wake up on a train to New Orleans?

Would you rather . . .

slide down a banister of razor blades into a pile of Cajun spice

or

be buried up to your neck and have your head used as a golf tee for a day?

Would you rather . . .

fight Mike Tyson

or

talk like him?

Would you rather . . .

be accomplished in the art of origami but be totally covered in moss

or

deeply understand the underlying themes of the *Porky's* saga but have the head of a Lego man?

Would you rather . . .

be able to wash/dry your clothes by wearing them

or

make your eyes glow red for a few seconds?

Would you rather live in a world . . .
where it rained Superballs

or

where people had Mr. Potato Head–style facial features that could be removed and exchanged?

If you could change history, would you rather . . .
add your name to the Declaration of Independence
or
preface the U.S. Constitution with "Freakazoids, please report to the dance floor"?

Would you rather know . . .

the specific date each person is going to die

or

the lyrics to every song made from 1975 to 1980?

Would you rather . . .
have a chest of thick poison oak

or

a sausage halo?

Would you rather have sex with . . .

Fred Flintstone or Barney Rubble?

Simon or Garfunkel?

Al Goldstein or the Hobbit?

Would you rather . . .

speak in the style, accent, and intensity of Hitler whenever talking to members of the opposite sex

or

have to take all your meals in a hockey net?

Would you rather . . .
experience a constant nagging sense of déjà vu
or
suffer from Ponchaphobia, the fear of Erik Estrada?

Would you rather . . .
have veins on the outside of your skin
or
have your mood directly dependent on how high your socks
are pulled up?
Things to consider: bathing depression

Would you rather . . .

vomit vehemently anytime you see someone named Klaus

or

experience a constant nagging sense of déjà vu?

Would you rather be stuck on a desert island with . . .
the Bible or a copy of *Juggs* magazine?

a Barry Manilow tape or a Rubik's Cube?

hungry cannibals or horny inmates?

avid Star Trek fans or constipated clowns?

Would you rather . . .

have a love of dance so insatiable that at the sound of any music you feel compelled to do the Conga (this stemming from your inability to control yourself any longa)

or

have an unbelievably extreme phobia of vegetables, rice, and anybody named Samuel?

Would you rather . . .

when asked where you come from, always answer, "Probably the creation of some insane wizard"

or

be incessantly preoccupied with the whereabouts of the Muffin Man?

Would you rather . . .

have a unique venereal disease where whenever you kiss someone they transform into a Japanese soldier who thinks the war is still on

or

have the inability to distinguish between the taste of mint and the concept of increasing?

Would you rather live in a world . . .

where all verbal exchange and written expression were conducted in Haiku

or

where a man's sexual prowess hinged entirely on the length of his mustache?

Things to consider: office memos, Rollie Fingers

Would you rather . . .

compulsively mumble, "Kibbles 'n Bits. Kibbles 'n Bits. I've got to get me some Kibbles 'n Bits" anytime you run or walk swiftly

or

have a condition whereupon becoming increasingly irritated, more and more popcorn starts to pop in your trousers?

You're searching through your child's private drawer. Would you rather find . . .

marijuana or a porno magazine?

heroin or S&M movies?

cocaine or lascivious pictures of Ralph Sampson?

Would you rather . . .
appear to be three feet to the left of where you really are

or

not exist on December 18 every year?

Would you rather . . .

have a purple cloud of dust appear when you flatulate

or

have a nervous compulsion whereupon meeting the parents of a date or spouse, you say quite happily, "Hello. How are you? Give me the salmon or I will destroy you"?

Would you rather . . .

have to always answer the phone with "I am the vindicator of the damned"

or

have a deep-seated insecurity that causes you to refer to yourself as "The Ambassador," as in "The Ambassador would like some more pie"?

Would you rather . . .

smile fiendishly and rub your hands together throughout all conversation

or

preface all of your statements with, "Beedy, beedy, beedy" like Twiki from Buck Rogers?

Things to consider: proposing marriage, seminars

Would you rather . . .

never be able to complete a thought

or